# Preserve Your Family Pictures

## How To Save Photo Heirlooms for Future Generations

By Amber Richards

# Table of Contents

Introduction ............................................................... 3

1. Identify and Preserve Family Photos ......................... 5

2. Salvage Pictures from Magnetic Photo Albums .......... 9

3. Attack the Storage Challenge ................................. 13

4. How to Avoid Deterioration of Photos ..................... 15

5. Organizing Your Family Pictures ............................ 17

6. What To Do in the Event of Water Damage ............. 19

7. Create Digital Copies ............................................. 23

8. Editing Pointers for Your Digital Photos .................. 29

9. Storage Suggestions for Digital Files ....................... 33

10. What About Slides? .............................................. 37

Conclusion ............................................................... 39

Copyright © Amber Richards 2014 All Rights Reserved. No part of this book may be reproduced without our express consent.

# Introduction

Thank you for downloading 'Preserve Your Family Pictures'. You have made a great choice to learn about how to protect the legacy of your family history, visually. It's something that not only will benefit you, but generations to come. What an amazing gift to offer them, and I'm sure it will be greatly appreciated.

If a person could only take one suitcase of their earthly belongings with them to their next destination, without the option of ever getting anything else, you can be sure that family photographs would be in that suitcase. They record our history, our loved ones, and are precious and irreplaceable.

As one who does photo restoration services (http://bellevuephotorestoration.com/), I have heard many tragic stories of the loss of family pictures. It's a sad sight to look into the eyes of one who's experienced that. It's a sadness that doesn't disappear with time, and it affects not only that person, but the rest of the family as well.

Some losses may be due to fire, water damage, mold, mildew, aging, theft or a host of other variables. We will be looking at both protecting and preserving your physical pictures, and well as digital formats. It's important to protect both forms from loss and damage.

Another aspect in family pictures is the case of a loved one that passes. There have been many family feuds over who inherits the photographs. If a family can agree to have one person undertake this process, copies of these treasures can then be made, for all family members to have and it benefit everyone.

This whole process can be a fascinating journey, you may be surprised at what you discover along the way. Let the journey begin.

# 1. Identify and Preserve Family Photos

Family pictures are an essential visual history of our ancestors, and helps us to connect with them. Similar familial traits, like hair, facial expressions, physical appearance, and more can many times be seen in the family line and can be enjoyable to discover. It is also interesting to observe clothing in eras past, and traditions that give us a glimpse of what is must have been like, in the lives of our ancestors. We must learn how to care for these precious pictures or we risk losing account of some of our history. These are irreplaceable!

Through the years, differing kinds of techniques have been utilized to produce photos. Collections of family pictures many times contain an intriguing blend of color formats and black & whites. Quite a few black & white pictures were made using silver fragments within a gelatin substance, or ointment, that was applied to the paper.

Colored pictures used various dyes to create the finished image. Usually many different types of methods can be found in picture collections ranging from large portraits, to snapshot photos. Older photos especially tend to be fragile, and may not last from the passing on of them to the next generation, so it is essential and urgent to save and store family pictures properly.

This book is written with the broad objective of guiding you on the practical steps of how to effectively save your family pictures, so your future descendants can enjoy and learn about their family history. This will most likely be a long process, so instead of working like a maniac doing 24 hours straight until your eyes are blurry and you can't think straight, consider finding time in your schedule for consistent, manageable chunks of time. You may want to dedicate half an hour a day to this project (or whatever time allows you and on the schedule right for you), just be consistent and steady, and it will be a completed project at some point, giving a sense of great satisfaction for an important job well done!

**Suggestions for Photo Preservation**

To pinpoint who or what the subject of the photo is about is one of the first steps that should be taken for preservation. A good way to do this is to write on the back of the photo gently, with a pen made for such a purpose. One such recommender marker is the Itoya Art Profolio Photo Marker.

This pen is an archival type marker, being acid free, non-toxic, photo safe and made specifically for this use, just ensure that the ink dries thoroughly (it does dry quickly), before putting other objects on it.

**Start with Identification**

To help in organizing data about the pictures, jot down as many specifics about the person or people in the photo, dates, place or the situation, as you can on the back of the picture. These details may be precious to those down the line, and the record of that information could be lost forever if you don't document it.

If you don't know that info, consider interviewing other family members to help in properly identifying these, this is a critical step in preserving history. Think of yourself as the family historian. Don't rush it in order to get done. If necessary, you might want to make a file of photographs that you need more data on, then when you interview other family members, show the whole folder to them to hoping get multiple answers. Keep searching until you get those questions answered.

**Handle with Care**

When working and handling pictures, a lot of care must be exercised. Oils from skin stay on the photos and lure dirt and grime, providing an ideal environment for mold to grow. It's a good idea to wear clean, white cotton gloves when handling photos. Gentle, even support should be used when handling pictures too, since older and weightier photos tend to become brittle with age, and can break quite easily. Handling in this way, helps to not damage fragile images.

## 2. Salvage Pictures from Magnetic Photo Albums

If you have photos in magnetic photo albums, now is the time to get them out. Leaving them in there will only cause further deterioration with time. The sooner the rescue process begins, the better success you will have in saving these pictures. These albums can cause damage in the following ways:

The materials used to make magnetic photo albums are acidic, starting with the cardboard. This causes the photo paper to deteriorate. The glue used on the adhesive pages are also acidic, giving pictures a double whammy. It causes with time, the pictures to become permanently stuck. This destroys both the pictures after they are detached, as well as any notes on the back. Lastly, the plastic sheets uses polyvinyl chloride that discharge a gas that effects the pictures by causing them to stick to these plastic sheets (sometimes permanently), crease, and fade out.

Start with a photo that means the least. I'll give you several examples of methods to try to remove them. On each method, go gently so as not to damage it more. If one method doesn't work, carefully try another, don't force it. If you can't safely remove them with any of the methods listed here, another option to try is to scan the photo, the entire album page in a scanner and digitize the image (see later in the book how). You could then have it re-printed to a physical photo.

Another option is to take your album to a photo store and have negatives made of your photos, then simply have new ones printed. Or, you could do this on only the photos that you couldn't successfully remove from the magnetic album. If you have the negatives of the pictures in the album, just having new ones printed might be your quickest route and best result, plus saving you the time and effort of getting them out undamaged.

The first step to salvage your pictures is to slowly and carefully try to peel the plastic cover off. If you can see by the attempt, that it has sealed to the photo and won't come off without ruining the picture, don't attempt anymore.

If you were able to get the plastic film off successfully, proceed with the other strategies. If one method doesn't work, try another. However, for each method use great care and if it doesn't come up easily, don't force it. If it's an extremely valuable photo, you might want to simply take it to a photo restorer and not even attempt it yourself.

Method 1 - Dental floss method; Use unwaxed dental floss, and gently slip it between the photo and the album and use a gentle sawing motion to lift the picture off the page.

Method 2 - Freezer. You can try to put the page you are working on in the freezer for about 5 - 10 minutes. It will help the glue to get brittle, and hopefully release the photo with ease. You don't want to leave it any longer however, as you don't want condensation forming. You may also want to try the dental floss method now.

Method 3 - Undo adhesive remover. This is a product used by many scrap bookers and is safe for the use on photos, however make sure you don't get any product on the image itself. It includes a tool to help you slip the product on to the back side of the photo to get it to lift up and off the album.

Method 4 - Thin metal spatula and hairdryer. This method involves the use of a thin metal spatula, art stores sell these. Heat the spatula a bit with a hairdryer. Be certain you don't let any heated air get on the photo. Once the spatula is heated somewhat, try gently slipping it in between the photo and the album. The heated spatula may help the glue to soften enough to release. Go slowly and carefully. You may need to reheat the spatula several times during this process.

Method 5 - Microwave. Place the album page you are working on in the microwave and heat for 5 seconds.
 Wait 10 seconds then zap another 5 seconds. Do this cycle several times, checking the glue each time. Do not do this in one 30 second session as it could burn the photo and damage it. Remove from the microwave and try to gently lift off, or use the dental floss method. The thought behind this procedure is to soften the adhesive enough to release the photo.

## 3. Attack the Storage Challenge

When thinking about storing photos, sometimes knowing what not to do can be as beneficial as knowing what to do. Don't use supplies such as tape, staples, rubber bands, paper clips, or glue on images as they can cause damage in the form of dentations, scratches or stains. Only 'acid free' cardboard, paper or other wood products should be used, as other types can damage pictures.

Even framing should be handled with care. Framed pictures should use acid free mats and backboards. The mat will help prevent the picture from touching the glass, thus reducing deterioration of this framed piece. Pictures should not be displayed in places where they receive direct sunlight.

Some other methods to store pictures involve using plastic sleeves that do not contain PVC, and can be bought at craft or photo supply stores. Some of these types might be in the form of photo albums with plastic sleeves that create 'pages'. This method not only stores your pictures in an organized manner, but is also a good way to view the photos. A strategy to store large amounts of pictures is to layer them in between pages of 100% acid free cotton bond paper, in an acid free storage box.

Acid free photo storage boxes are a great way of storing photos as these boxes are made specifically for this use. There are many sizes, types and brands that can be found. Some contain smaller compartments within for organizational purposes. This is a good route for those that perhaps have no intentions of putting the photos in some type of album, yet keeps them safe.

## 4. How to Avoid Deterioration of Photos

By exercising care when choosing a location of where to store your photos, you will greatly reduce the deterioration of the pictures. The ideal storage temperate is 68 degrees, and keeping the humidity around 30-40%, in a stable environment. This isn't always possible to achieve, but do your best to think in these terms, when choosing a place for storage. Extreme fluctuations of temperature, humidity, expose to sunlight, dust & dirt are all very damaging conditions and will reduce the life of the pictures.

Unfavorable, settings to keep your family pictures are basements, attics, un-insulated garages or storage units. Is there an interior closet of the home, that might be a good option? If there is, ensure that it is not close to a water heater, pipes, shower or other water sources that could get the pictures wet, if they broke.

Certain weather conditions can cause pictures to become brittle and prone to cracking and breaking. Hot and humid summer weather, then cold and dry winter weather are the harshest conditions. In extremes situations, the images can actually begin to separate from the paper backing of the photos.

These are not the only enemies to battle to preserve your pictures. Photos may tend to stick together if they are exposed to damp conditions. Rodents, and some types of bugs also feed off photos or use them for nesting material.

The ideal storage location isn't always possible in a home environment. A good alternative might be storing them in a safe deposit box at your bank where the environment is stable and secure.

Storing photo negatives in the same location as the photos is not a good idea. If a disaster, theft or some other kind of damage affected the photos, those negatives would suffer the same fate the photos did, and possibly be destroyed forever. You've then lost your backups as well. Consider having a friend or family member store your negatives, or keep them in a bank safe deposit box. If you do not have negatives of your original photos, consider investing in having them made, this provides another level of safety in the preservation process.

There is a tendency to both display our most important pictures, and think

they are safe in doing so. Not only does a photo fade in sunlight, but the glass can stick to the picture over time, making it impossible to remove. A better way to do this is to frame a copy of the picture, then ensure the original photo is in safe storage.

## 5. Organizing Your Family Pictures

Sometimes figuring out a system to organize your pictures can be the most difficult part. In the most basic, bare bones way however, is whatever method makes the most sense to you, works. Here we'll provide some suggestions, although you may find you favor one over another, or a unique combination. There's no wrong way here.....except by not doing anything at all.

For some folks, grouping images by size works well. By getting archival quality plastic bags or sheets, they can easily be prepared for storage in this way.

Other people prefer to sort the photos by date. Depending on the volume of pictures you have, it might be a year's worth, or a decade's worth of images per section. Similarly if you have a good amount of photos from a certain event, it would make sense to store those together.

Another method or organizing that might be beneficial, especially when there is a large, extended family represented, is to sort by nuclear family members.

Some individuals opt to use archival quality photo albums with acid free pages and acid free corner tab mounts. Not only would this preserve the photos nicely, it would be visually appealing to take a journey down memory lane with. The one drawback to this however, is that is can be expensive because of the high quality of materials used. Perhaps this could be reserved for the most favored images, or as budget allows.

While you are in this process, it is ok to toss photos that are junk. These might be landscape photos from a vacation years ago that you have no idea where the place even is, and it's not particularly pretty or special in any way. It may be a childhood crush in which you can't even remember their name or who this person is.
There is no reason to keep something that means nothing to you, or doesn't depict basic family history.

In more recent decades a lot of the family pictures were taken in color. Color pictures however most likely won't last more than about 50 years or so, although experts seem to have varied opinions on exactly how many. It is important that these be properly stored and cared for as well. It might be a good idea to have re-prints made of these from the negatives every 30 years or so.

Most pictures available now are usually either 3 ½ x 5" or 4x6". Since these are common sizes currently, pocket sleeves made from plastic (be sure to use archival quality plastic sleeves) can be easily found. Some also have areas designated for writing data about the photos. Do this for future generations so they won't have the same problems you are encountering now.

## 6. What To Do in the Event of Water Damage

What happens if you discover photos that have water damage? It might be possible to salvage them, if they are discovered soon and action is taken quickly.

First assess if there are undamaged negatives of these pictures. If they exist, the easiest fix is to simply have new photos printed from the negatives, and not waste time and effort trying to save the wet photos.

The photos for which no negatives exist should get your attention and care first. If the pictures have attached to each other, or if mold is growing on them, there might not be anything that can rescue them.

Use great caution when handling the wet images as they are very fragile.

Consider using a good quality digital camera to take a close-up picture of the wet picture, at the earliest point that you can see a clear image. This might be the only possible 'save' if the condition gets worse and no negative exists. It might be able to be recovered digitally.

Gently attempt to peel images stuck to glass, or mats without damaging it further. If that is unsuccessful, and the picture is in pretty good shape, you can scan it from your scanner in the glass. Then any fixes beyond that could be sent to a photo restorer (if you can't do it yourself) for repair digitally and then reprinted.

To remove a wet photo from the picture frame, keep the glass and photo together, removing it from the frame. Take hold of the picture and glass together, rinse with gently flowing water from the tap, allowing the water stream to separate glass from the image. Carefully lay the picture on a clean, white towel to dry.

If you have photos in an album, or a stack of loose photos covered with mud or muddy water, gently rinse each photo front & back with clear flowing water. Lay flat to dry on clean towels. After they are thoroughly dry, if they have curled, put in between heavy books overnight to flatten. It's a good idea to put them in between acid free paper first, so they don't come into direct contact with the books.

If you have several photos stuck together you can try one of these two methods. This is for actual print photographs however, not digitally printed images.

Soaking Method - submerge the photos in a bowl of room temperature water and wait about 10 minutes. See if you can easily pull them apart. If not, you can soak these for a few hours, up to overnight. Change the water every couple of hours however, so you are dealing with clean water. Remove the photos from the water, they should be unstuck. Lay flat on a towel to dry. If edges curl after it is dry, place in between a couple of heavy books to flatten.

Before we move on to the realm of digital photos and having your family pictures made to digital format, let's look at some other options having to do with all these photos you now have.

You have the images for many years of amazing gifts at your fingertips. This may be a time to take up scrap booking as a hobby. There is so much to that topic, you'll probably want to read up and study before beginning. You may want to have a few copies made of your photos, to share with family and friends. You may want to frame a few both for yourself and relatives. These will make special gifts for holidays, birthdays or any other special occasion. Yearly calendars can also be made for family members, using new photos every year.

## 7. Create Digital Copies

In today's technology, there's so much more available concerning photographs than in generations past. It is a wise thing to go through the process of having your family pictures converted to digital files. A couple of reasons for this would be the creativity options it opens up for you and future generations, as well as providing another level of preserving these images from loss, aging, theft or other disasters.

Digital formats also make sharing with other family members and friends much easier and cost efficient. Those family members could have physical copies made of only the photos they want, in the size and quantities they desire.

If you are technology challenged, consider enlisting the help of younger family members. It could be an incredibly bonding experience between generations, the process of converting these family heirlooms to digital. Many memories and stories could be shared in this joint effort. The other option if you don't want to personally do this, is to hire it done. There are many companies out there who can scan your photos to discs for you.

Another option is that most public libraries teach free classes on how to digitize your physical photos. Most also have the equipment like a good scanner that can be used as well, for those that do not have one nor wish to purchase their own.

I'd like to offer a point of caution at this time. If you are having any business or individual work in some way with your collection of family pictures for various services, if they are using your original photos, do it in batches. Most are very careful and reputable, but there can be rare instances that some emergency or something extraordinary happens (or if they were shipped, the shipment got lost) that your pictures could be lost or damaged. By doing the work in batches, you are not putting every single photo of your entire collection at risk. It would be terrible to lose a batch of photos, but catastrophic to lose every single one!

**Tips for Scanning & Restoring**

We will share some very basic information when it comes to creating and editing digital photos. The degree to which you delve into this aspect really depends on your computer and Photoshop or other photo editing software skills, your willingness to learn, and how far you want to take it. This aspect can quickly become very complex and advanced, and is not within the intended scope of this book. If you have a desire to learn more about digital photo restoration, there are many excellent resources out there to expand your knowledge of this topic. Who knows, maybe you'll even find a new hobby! These skills would certainly open many options for a very creative aspect in your family picture project.

Having your photos in a digital format makes it easy for sharing these photos with other family members and friends, posting to websites if you want, making digital scrapbooks or having those scrapbooks printed to hard copy. The strongest reason however to convert your photos to digital, is giving you another, stronger level of protection for saving these heirlooms for future generations.

You'll want to invest in a good scanner (or use one at the local public library). They aren't that expensive. Some are single flat bed scanners, or you can opt for a 3 in 1 printer that has scanning ability, a fax and printer. Once you have your scanner set up and ready to go, we will begin the process of scanning your images to a digital file. Try scanning as a test, just a regular piece of paper with something written on it, so you can see how it works, adjust any settings that might need adjusting and to see how the scanned item looks in general.

Before you start scanning, you want to make sure the scanner glass is pristine clean. You can use either a cleanser that's used for cleaning camera lenses, or regular glass cleaner, but DO NOT put any cleaning product directly on the glass. Apply it sparingly to a lint free clean white cloth and gently wipe the glass thoroughly until it both clean and dry. It's a good idea to wait 10- 15 minutes or so before scanning to guarantee that the glass is completely dry. You don't want any of this product to get onto your pictures.

It's recommended you wear clean, white cotton gloves for your hands when doing some scanning. Check your images for smudges, lint, dust or dirt. Take either a super soft, clean brush, or dry lint-free photo-wipes and gently sweep away. Place the photos, one at a time, face down on your scanner glass, and close the lid. Some scanners have the feature of 'batch scanning', in which several images can be scanned at once, then it saves each image in that batch, with it's own file. If your scanner doesn't have the batch feature, you'll be scanning each image one at a time, so that each image becomes it's own file.

When scanning photos, you'll have a basic choice of color photo versus black and white. When scanning family photos, it is usually best to scan in color, even if the source photo is black & white. You'll have more manipulation options this way, and you can change a color photo to black & white (grayscale), but not the other way around.

You will then want to decide what resolution you want to scan your images in, both for the quality and usefulness in the future. This is one topic where you will find a very wide range of opinions on. It may be a subject that you might like to study more in depth. In general however, a good rule of thumb is 300 dpi (dots per inch). This will be a setting on your scanner that it asks you to choose. This figure gives a good amount a detail without being an overly large file.

Gently place your photo(s) face down on the scanner glass, do your best to ensure that it is straight and no portion will be cut off. Close the lid and then hit 'prescan' or 'preview' button. At this preview stage, make sure everything looks correct. If you need to straighten a photo, you can open the lid and re-position it now and close the lid.

If your scanner has the option of cropping to only the photo, do that now. If it doesn't, you can also crop later if you desire. Some scanners do this step automatically.

Go ahead and hit scan. It shouldn't take very long. When it's done a window will pop up, click 'save as' and name the file something that will make it easy for you to identify what it is, and save to the location on your computer that you want.

On your computer where you will be saving your pictures, create folders and sub-folders that help you place, and later locate your digital files. They might be a date range, an event, family members or any other category you want. It makes sense to make it a system similar to the organizational system of the physical prints. This is very important, and please give some thought to it beforehand, as this can save you and others many hours in the future, searching for a particular photo. It has to make sense to you.

## 8. Editing Pointers for Your Digital Photos

Having the ability to edit your digital photos is a great skill to have. If you don't possess those skills you can either opt to hire photo editing done, skip it altogether, or learn how. Below we'll go into the 3$^{rd}$ option, tips to help you learn how, although these will be very basic fixes. Complete photo editing can be quite complex and depending what the goal is, can be difficult to master.

A couple of common programs used for photo editing are Photoshop, Photoshop elements (a simpler and more economic version) and lightroom, although there are many more.

I found when I first began using Photoshop elements, it didn't seem user intuitive to me. I couldn't seem to do even very basic things. I read some how-to books, but even they were beyond my beginning skill level. Ultimately, I ended up taking a course at a local community college and it and it was the best thing ever! I got the basics down, was able to ask questions live, see the answers, duplicate the tasks, and ask more questions as I was doing this hands-on. After the course, I was then able to gain knowledge from other books, and Utube tutorials.

One of the main reasons for doing photo editing is that every photo can look better with even minor editing. We're not talking editing that changes the photo so much you can't even tell what the original was about. It's about enhancing and bringing out the best.

Ok, so now we'll dive into some basic tips you may want to do on your digital photos.

1. Open in your photo editing software the image that you want to work on. Create a copy of the original of this file by clicking 'file/save as/ then save in the area on your computer you want it saved. This will be the copy you will work on, and the original will be left untouched. You always want to work from a copy, never the original. Keep an original untouched as well, so you can start over if you make a mistake.

2. You may want to crop your photo using the crop tool. If you had the image scanned within a frame, you'll want the frame cropped out. Cropping a photo can also make the composition of the picture more visually appealing. Depending upon your purpose, you may also wish to use the crop tool to cut out the background or focus in on a particular person. This can make a world of difference in the look of an image, many times backgrounds are too busy or cluttered and they actually detract from the main subject of the image. Cropping closer around a person also makes it look as though the person is closer to the camera.

3. If any of the people in the photo have red eyes, you can remove that. You can remove that with the automatic red eye removal tool. You click on that tool to activate it, then click on the red eye you want fixed, one at a time. Sometimes it will alter the original eye color. If this happens, it

requires a more complex fix.

4. Correct the contrast and colors in your image. It is common that aging photos have discolored, yellowed, faded or darkened. Some of these flaws may have also been there at the point the photograph was originally taken. There are usually some lighting issues that can also improve the picture's quality.

   a. Lighting - In Photoshop Elements go to Enhance/adjust lighting/shadows & highlights. This window allows you to lighten up dark shadow areas of the photo, and darken other areas that are too light. You can play with the adjustments to find what seems best. It also allows you to adjust the mid tone contrast as well. These simple tweaks using the slider bars will really help your picture's overall appearance.

   b. Color - Remove odd color casts and increase saturation. Both of these will dramatically increase your image's appeal. This is where you'll rid the picture of yellowing and any other discolored issues, and the fading. In Photoshop Elements go to Enhance/adjust color/remove color cast. A window will open along with an 'eyedropper' icon. You want to tap this eyedropper in a section of the picture that is supposed to be black, white or gray. I usually try to aim for white first. If that doesn't look correct, keep clicking the eyedropper around for black or gray areas, until you get a natural looking color. Many times this is a dramatic step because the discoloration can be so pronounced.

Once it is where you are happy with at this phase, next go to 'Enhance/adjust color/adjust hue saturation' a window will appear and you'll slide the slider bar for saturation up 10 - 25 is quite usual, but adjust it to look good to your preference. This is what compensates for the fading picture. Save your work.

Doing these minor repairs on your pictures will improve their appearance immensely. There are many other editing effects (and methods) that can always be added if desired, along with creative artistic effects. Photo editing is a skill that is very useful to have and enjoyable for many people to do. At times it seems as though a person could never learn all there is to know on this topic. Have fun, keep learning, or hire someone to get it done.

## 9. Storage Suggestions for Digital Files

Storage for your digital files are critical for safe keeping for future generations. Especially since more and more, this is the direction technology is moving. Electronic photo albums are used commonly and there's no telling what new advances in this realm will be invented later for the purposes of displaying photos. Think of this as the process of securing your original photos, plan that these will outlive your physical pictures.

More caution needs to be taken rather than simply burning your files to a CD and tossing in a drawer. Even in a stable environment, CDs only last about 5 years and then they start to deteriorate. If that happens, when you put your CD in your computer to try to look at your pictures, you'll get an error message about not being able to read files, and they are gone.

Many people don't want their photos on their computer hard drives because of the space it takes up and if your hard drive crashes, you may lose all your photos.

One very good option is to buy an external hard drive to store your photos on. For those that don't know what this is, it's a device that you plug into your computer for the purpose of data storage in other words a separate place to store your digital photos. You should also have this external hard drive backed up as well. Once you have your files loaded onto one of these, it might be a good idea to store them in a bank deposit box. This is protection from theft, fires, or other disasters that could strike at home.

A second option is a web-based data storage solution, sometimes known as a 'cloud'. In a nutshell, this is a place where your images are stored online. As long as you have an internet connection, you can log on to your account from any computer to retrieve your images. There are many companies that offer this type of service and usually the fee is fairly low. You can set these up so only you have access, or specific people if you want to, they don't have to be available to the general public. A couple of such sites are Flickr and Shutterfly, but there are many out there to choose from.

They also allow you to organize your images into albums for easy sorting. I've used Shutterfly many times for having my photos printed and they do a great job, so that's another bonus. Once your photos are stored there, at any point you can easily go order any prints you want at reasonable prices and good quality. I've got to mention another feature at Shutterfly I love, photo books! You can design quickly and easily a photo book, you choose which images you want in a page, how many per page, the background, soft bound or hard copy, and they will create your photo book and mail it to you. These make incredible gifts and are a good alternative to scrapbooking or other photo albums. Frequently they run sales and specials for photo books too, so do a web search for 'Shutterfly coupon codes' to see what kind of deals you can find.

Given the value of your digital photos, it is highly recommended to implement both methods for the extra levels of protection they provide.

Here are some practical tips for the storage and saving

digital files process:

Choose an archival method, and use a good photo editing program. Using the TIF (tagged imaged format) option for saving your images is by far the best format to go with. The reason for this is that it is considered loss-less, in other words the data is preserved. TIF files are larger than JPG files. Other formats such as JPEG or JPG are common, but the compression done to make the files smaller, may cause some quality loss of the data in the file. One recommendation is to do all your archival saving in TIF, then if you want to print or share those images, make a copy to JPG for that use, but always retain and consider your TIF images to be your archival files, with the intention that it will outlast the original physical photographs.

Digital files are also so great for sharing pictures with family and friends. CDs or DVDs can be burned and shared with the digital pictures contained on the disc. The recipients can then download those photos to their computers, external hard drives or web based storage. Smaller JPG files can also be emailed to family, or posted on sites like Facebook if desired.

## 10. What About Slides?

Many people have hundreds, if not thousands of slides that need to be considered for preservation as well.

These should be saved in the same way that physical photographs should be, clearly identified and stored in archival quality boxes in the same ideal climate conditions. If any plastic is used, be sure it is the non-PVC type, made for photographic use, acid free materials for archival purposes.

Some people choose to digitize their slides as well. Some scanners have accessories that can be used for scanning slides. It is a good idea to get these converted for more protection of these slides. There are businesses who can also do the scanning of your slides for you, if you prefer. If you go down this route, do it in batches.

Slides were a technology that were very popular not that long ago, but seem to be slowly fading away. There are many in the next generation who have never seen a slide, nor have any idea of what they are. How long has it been that you've pulled out the slide projector to view those slides? With the wave of new technology, it's anyone's guess to what the future will hold. Projectors may get more difficult to find or have repaired, and getting slides made into prints may prove harder to find businesses to do those services, and may cost much higher prices to have done. I've also seen businesses who offer the service of both scanning your slides to digital format, and provide you with physical prints of these images.

Consider having your slides printed to physical photographs now, and put in archival photo albums or displayed in frames to enjoy. Chances are these have not been seen as much as the print photographs in your family have been. It may be like having brand new pictures of times past. Any that you don't put in albums or frames, archive in the same way as the other print photographs.

Don't throw your original slides away however, even after you have them digitized and/or printed.

# Conclusion

Although it may seem like a daunting task at this point, to properly preserve your family pictures, slides and digitize your collection, don't allow procrastination to take over. If this is not followed up by action, you are no closer to saving your photos than before. There is just too much at stake, not only for you, but for your descendents to enjoy their family history in pictures. This is a portion of their inheritance. Even though you might not ever be personally thanked for your hard work, know that it will be greatly appreciated in the years to come.

Try to enjoy the process and enlist as much help from other family members as possible in this labor of love project.

If you enjoyed this book or received value from it in any way, would you be kind enough to leave a review for this book on Amazon? I would be so grateful. Thank you!

Printed in Dunstable, United Kingdom